Editor
Eric Migliaccio

Managing Editor
Ina Massler Levin, M.A.

Editor-in-Chief
Sharon Coan, M.S. Ed.

Illustrator
Kevin McCarthy

Cover Artist
Brenda DiAntonis

Art Manager
Kevin Barnes

Art Director
CJae Froshay

Imaging
Richard E. Easley

Product Manager
Phil Garcia

Publisher
Mary D. Smith, M.S. Ed.

High Frequency Word Practice

Author

Ruth Foster, M. Ed.

Teacher Created Resources, Inc.
6421 Industry Way
Westminster, CA 92683
www.teachercreated.com
ISBN 13: 978-0-7439-3705-4
ISBN 10: 0-7439-3705-8
©2004 Teacher Created Resources, Inc.
Reprinted, 2006
Made in U.S.A.

Table of Contents

Introduction

It is a given that children attend school to learn how to read. It is a further given that every teacher wants to teach all of his or her students in the classroom to learn how to read. Yet one does not have to visit very many kindergarten and first-grade classes to realize that not every child learns to read in the same way or at the same rate.

There are some students who excel at learning words phonetically, stringing together the sounds of individual sounds to form words. There are other students who have yet to understand or grasp the connection between a letter and its sound. There might be some of the students who learn their first words by the visual shape of the total word—its length, lines, circles, and up and down extensions. They develop the phonetic connection after they have learned to recognize the word.

High Frequency Word Practice provides a series of exercises that allows a teacher to work with children of varying levels and different learning styles in a group setting or on an individual basis. These exercises reinforce letter and vowel identification and letter formation and sequence. They develop visual memory, improve visual-auditory perception, reinforce word comprehension, and provide practice with rhyming sounds and word writing.

The breadth of the exercises in *High Frequency Word Practice* allows children with different learning styles to add to their strengths and develop their weaknesses. Skills practiced and developed in the *High Frequency Word Practice* exercises will carry over to the successful expansion of students' reading vocabulary.

How to Use this Book

A teacher may choose to use this book while working with the entire class, in small groups, or one on one with particular students. If the teacher goes through these exercises with the class as a whole, he or she can write the correct answers on the board, allowing the students to self-correct.

Word exercises may also be assigned as homework or as extra practice and reinforcement for words covered in the classroom. The word exercises provide a specific and structured task with a clear beginning and end that parents and children can easily follow.

The flashcards at the back of the book can be sent home as each word is covered in school to provide additional practice for the student.

Word Choice

Words for this book were chosen from a variety of sight-word lists. Factors that determined word choice were: rank on high frequency word lists, rhyming possibilities, phonics reinforcement practice, long and short vowel practice, and introduction of rules such as "the silent *e* makes the vowel say its name."

The *wh* words—*what, where, when, why, who,* and *which*—were all included. These words were chosen not just because they are all on the sight word lists, but because many beginning readers have trouble visually differentiating these words when they are first introduced.

Missing Words

Due to space limitations, many high frequency words are not in this book. An arbitrary decision was made in several instances not to include a particular word because exercises were provided for another high frequency sight word that was very similar. For example, the words *all*, *call*, and *ball*, and *could*, *would*, and *should* are on many high frequency word lists. Although only exercise sheets for *all*, *could*, and *would* are included, an introduction to and practice with the missing high frequency words occurs within the covered sight word exercises during rhyming exercises or in the Creature Challenge supplementary exercises.

Making Your Own New Word Exercises

Blank New Word Forms for making one's own exercise sheets are provided at the back of the book (pages 136 and 137). A teacher can easily fill in the forms for a specific word that he or she wishes to cover on a particular day. For example, a teacher may want to provide additional practice on a geography or social studies term he or she is introducing, or he or she may find it prudent to reinforce new sight words in the upcoming reading assignments.

It has been said that true mastery comes when one can teach a concept. The New Word Forms have been designed so that a student can write his or her own new word lesson. After filling out the exercise sheets (in class or as homework), the student can complete his or her own exercises or trade them with a fellow student so that each can complete a new lesson.

Allowing the student to play the role of instructor will help a child practice with and gain mastery over a new word. Confidence and self-esteem may rise simply due to the fact that as a child discovers that he or she is capable of making up his or her own exercises, the exercises, even those they did not write, become more familiar and less intimidating.

A teacher may also choose to request a child to fill in a New Word Form on rhyming words or words with different endings. For example:

- after the exercises for the sight words *fun* or *funny* are gone over in class, a teacher may request that a child make exercises for the words *sun*, *bun*, *run*, *sunny*, *bunny*, or *runny*.
- after the exercises for the words *some* and *thing* are gone over in class, a teacher may request a child to fill in a New Word Form for the word *something*.
- after the exercises for the sight word *look*, a teacher may assign some students to fill in New Word Forms for the words *looks*, *looked*, and *looking*.

Word and Exercise Order

Words can be taught in any order. They are not listed in order of importance or difficulty. They are listed alphabetically for reference convenience. A teacher may choose a particular word lesson because of its beginning sound, vowel sound, rhyming possibilities, or placement in a reading lesson.

Exercises always follow the same order and format. A teacher may decide to skip a particular exercise if he or she does not feel it is appropriate for the class.

The Exercises

Tracing the Word

Tracing the word allows the student to be introduced to the new sight word in a non-threatening manner. The student becomes familiar with the letters making up the word and their sequence. There is the secondary benefit of letter formation practice.

Finding the Box

Asking a child to find the box that the word fits into allows the child to focus on the entire word shape, or *gestalt*, of the word. This activity forces a child to think about how the letters fit against each other—whether there are letters that go above or below the line, and whether those upward and downward letters go at the beginning of the word or at the end.

Circling the Word's Letters from the Alphabet

This seemingly simple activity is important on several levels. It reinforces alphabet sequence while providing an exercise in visual matching. Most importantly, it helps a child realize that language is manageable. Every word is going to be formed from these same 26 letters—regardless of the number of letters a word contains and what the letters are. It develops within a child a sense that language is a code with a finite number of pieces. New words will be assemblages of the code pieces.

Filling in the Missing Letters

Requiring a child to fill in missing letters allows a child to develop an awareness of letter sequence without being overwhelmed by the task. It reinforces the understanding that every letter is needed to make up a word and that the letter must appear in a particular order. It aids in spelling mastery, as well as providing the secondary benefit of letter formation practice.

Circling the Vowels

As with circling the word's letters from the alphabet, this activity is important on several levels. Obviously it reinforces vowel identification, but it also helps to develop the sense that the language code (reading) has rules. Every word requires at least one vowel. Although circling the vowels may not seem that important when sight words are introduced, familiarity with vowels will help during later phonics exercises, syllabication, and spelling.

Fixing Spelling Errors

During this exercise, a child is given the authority to be the "doctor." It is a given that the word is spelled incorrectly. It is up to the child to fix it. By having to fix the word several times, each time identifying a different error, proper spelling is reinforced. To many students, the idea of fixing something is what maintains their interest. They enjoy crossing out wrong letters and inserting correct ones. In addition, this exercise aids in developing editing skills. Checking that one has used the correct vowel and letter formation (*b* versus *d*, for example), provides practice for the types of things that a child will look for when he or she is self-correcting his or her own work later on. A teacher may want to instruct the children on the use of the caret (^), the editing symbol for the insertion of a letter, at this time. Rewriting the word entirely is optional.

The Exercises *(cont.)*

Beginning Letters and Rhyming

This guided exercise where students are given beginning letters to put in front of word roots to create a list of rhyming words (*cat*, *bat*, *fat*, *pat*, and *sat*, for example) reinforces letter sounds and allows the students to practice rhyming in a non-threatening way. It also enables the child to see patterns with words, reinforcing same sounding endings such as *ake*, *ook*, *ing*, and *ay*.

Circling the Correctly Spelled Word

A child is expected to identify the correctly spelled sight word out of a list of five words. This exercise frees a child from the physical constraints of writing and allows him or her to focus instead on the visual aspect of writing. It helps a child to develop a mental image of the word and provides reinforcement practice for word image memorization.

Writing Practice

Writing the word twice, once with eyes open and once with eyes shut, has a two-fold purpose. When the eyes are open, it allows a child to practice word writing and focus on penmanship, spacing, and spelling. When his or her eyes are closed, a child is freed from concern over neatness. It is fun, of course, to see if one can write as well with one's eyes open as shut, but the primary focus of this exercise is to strengthen a child's mental visual image of a word. Transcribing the brain's word image down on paper reinforces the visual image, thus building retention of word recognition and spelling. This also provides an opportunity for those children who learn kinesthetically, or by feel, to concentrate on their hand motions as they write. It takes very different movements to form the letter *s*, for example, as opposed to the letter *i*.

Language Context Question

In this exercise, a simple question using the new word is asked. The child is not expected to read the question or answer it on paper. Instead, the child listens to the adult read the question so that he or she can hear the new sight word being used in a real language situation. By interspersing oral discussion with written work, the child begins to develop a sense that the language code is a continuum of reading, writing, comprehension, and speaking. It is more than identifying letters and reading.

Creature Challenge

The creatures Counting Crow, Detective Dog, Rhyming Rhino, and Vowel Vixen are used to supplement the exercises with a question. These questions are optional. It is not expected that a new reader be able to read them. Rather, they are to be listened to. The questions each creature asks can range from what vowels say their names, to number of syllables in a word, to words that though they rhyme, are not spelled in a consistent pattern. These supplementary exercises are not crucial to the learning of a new sight word, but they introduce concepts that students will soon be coming across as their reading skills develop.

Counting Crow

Detective Dog

Rhyming Rhino

Vowel Vixen

The Exercises (cont.)

The Language Context Question and the Creature Challenge exercises have been placed at the end of the worksheet. This strategic location ensures that there is a clear and visible stopping point for students who have been assigned to fill in parts of the worksheets on their own. A teacher may choose to bring up the Language Context Question or the Creature Challenge at any time, thereby fitting active discussion to the class schedule and interest, the need to refocus children on task, or personal preference.

> **Selected Answers to Language Context Questions:** all (no); big (bicycle); book (dictionary); boy (stallion); cat (cat); dog (bark); end (start); girl (filly, hen, cow, does); look (telescope); red (orange—red and blue make purple); saw (crows = caw, owls = hoot); that (all spiders have eight legs); thing (caterpillar); when (morning); where (Earth, face, store, 23rd, bed); who (cow, zoologist, paleontologist, architect, forester); why (to chew our food).

Auditory Reinforcement

Retention of the word being taught will be greatly enhanced with auditory reinforcement. Although there are no specific directions as to when to have students repeat the words, a teacher can easily add oral word repetition to the exercises. He or she may:

- start the lesson by having the students repeat the word a set number of times. (A side benefit of this can be practice with number sense, especially if the teacher writes the number of times he or she wants the word said on the board.)
- intersperse the lesson with directions to recite the word a set number of times. This allows a manual rest between exercises and aids in the development of a visual and auditory connection.
- after the Beginning Letters and Rhyming section have the students read all of the rhyming words in unison. Reading these words out loud will reinforce, fine-tune, or help develop a child's auditory perception.
- request students to write the word in the air while they state the word, name each letter as they make the air motions, and then restate the word when they are done.
- when appropriate, have students read in unison the extra words in the supplementary Creature Challenge questions.
- end the lesson with, "What word did we just learn how to read?"

The number of times a teacher should encourage word repetition will depend greatly on the level of the class or individual student and difficulty of the word. It may well vary from 25 to 50 times. A teacher might desire a greater number of repetitions if he or she has, for example, filled out a New Word Form and is teaching a new vocabulary word.

all

Trace the word **all**.

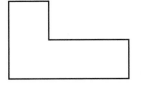 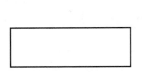 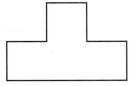 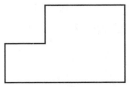

Find the box the word **all** fits into. Write **all** in the correct box.

Circle the letters from the alphabet found in the word **all**.

a b c d e f g h i j k l m n o p q r s t u v w x y z

Fill in the missing letters for the word **all**.

a _ l   _ l l   a l _
a _ _   _ l l   _ _ l

Circle the vowel in the word **all**. The vowels are: a, e, i, o, u.

Fix these words so they spell **all**.

oll   alle   aall   al   lla

all

You can make new words when you put letters in front of all.
What words do you make when you put these letters in front of all?

b	c	f	h	t	w

___ all   ___ all   ___ all

___ all   ___ all   ___ all

Circle the word all.

lla   all   lal   all   oll

Can you write the word all with your eyes open and closed?

Extension
• In the fall, do all the trees lose their leaves?

"Count, count! Put your hand under your chin. Count the number of times your chin hits your hand when you say these words. Do all the words have the same number of syllables?"

all
ball
cal
fall
wall
tall

and

Trace the word **and**.

and   and   and

Find the box the word **and** fits into. Write **and** in the correct box.

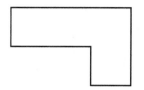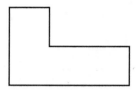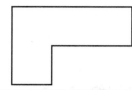

Circle the letters from the alphabet found in the word **and**.

a b c d e f g h i j k l m n o p q r s t u v w x y z

Fill in the missing letters for the word **and**.

a _ d   _ n d   a n _

a _ _   _ _ d   _ n _

Circle the vowel in the word **and**. The vowels are: a, e, i, o, u.

a   n   d

Fix these words so they spell **and**.

nd   amd   anb   end   anp

and

You can make new words when you put letters in front of **and**.
What words do you make when you put these letters in front of **and**?

b	h	l	s	gr	st

_____ a n d   _____ a n d   _____ a n d

_____ a n d   _____ a n d   _____ a n d

Circle the word **and**.

and   anb   amd   end   anp

Can you write the word **and** with your eyes open and closed?

Extension
- Do you like cats or dogs?
- Do you like cats and dogs?

"Help, help! I have lost the letter d. What does the word **and** become when it loses its d?

and

an

and

an

and

are

Trace the word **are**.

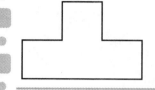   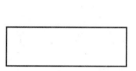   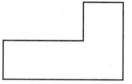   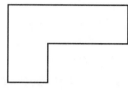

Find the box the word **are** fits into. Write **are** in the correct box.

Circle the letters from the alphabet found in the word **are**.

a b c d e f g h i j k l m n o p q r s t u v w x y z

Fill in the missing letters for the word **are**.

a _ e   _ r e   a r _

a _ _   _ r _   _ _ e

Circle the vowel in the word **are**. The vowels are: a, e, i, o, u.

a   r   e

Fix these words so they spell **are**.

era   arm   ar   aro   re

are

Circle the letter that says its name in the word **are**.

a r e

Listen to these sentences. What two sentences need the word **are**?

He _____ tall. We _____ tall.

The dog _____ small. The dogs _____ small.

Circle the word **are**.

ore   ame   ar   re   r   are

Can you write the word **are** with your eyes open and closed?

Extension
- Are you a cat, dog, or person?
- Are you a boy or are you a girl?

"Extra, extra! "I have a lot of
words that rhyme with **are**. They
are spelled a little differently. Can
you read them?"

are

car

far

jar

star

around

Trace the word **around**.

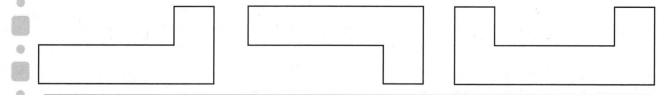

Find the box the word **around** fits into. Write **around** in the correct box.

Circle the letters from the alphabet found in the word **around**.

a b c d e f g h i j k l m n o p q r s t u v w x y z

Fill in the missing letters for the word **around**.

_ r o u n _   a _ o _ n _

_ r o u _ _   a r _ _ n d

Circle the vowels in the word **around**. The vowels are: a, e, i, o, u.

a   r   o   u   n   d

Fix these words so they spell **around**.

arounb   aroumb   aruond   round

around

Put **ar** in front of **ound**, and you make the word **around**.
What words do you make when you put these letters in front of **ound**?

f	h	m	p	r	s

___ o u n d   ___ o u n d   ___ o u n d

___ o u n d   ___ o u n d   ___ o u n d

Circle the word **around**.

round   aruond   arounb   around

Can you write the word **around** with your eyes open and closed?

Extension

• Does it take you longer to walk around your school or around your home?

"Count, count! I want to know which one of these words has two syllables. Put your hand under your chin. Say the word. What word makes your chin hit your hand two times?"

sound

found

round

around

pound

away

Trace the word **away**.

away   away   away

Find the box the word **away** fits into. Write **away** in the correct box.

Circle the letters from the alphabet found in the word **away**.

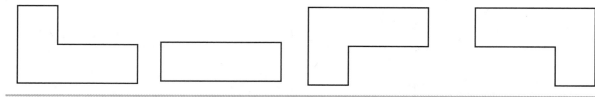

a b c d e f g h i j k l m n o p q r s t u v w x y z

Fill in the missing letters for the word **away**.

a _ a y   a w a _   a _ a _

_ w _ y   a _ _ y   _ w a _

Circle the vowel in the word **away**. The vowels are: a, e, i, o, u.

a   w   a   y

Fix these words so they spell **away**.

way   amay   oway   awy

away

Put **aw** in front of **ay**, and you make the word **away**.
What words do you make when you put these letters in front of **ay**?

d	h	l	p	s	w

_____ay   _____ay   _____ay

_____ay   _____ay   _____ay

Circle the word **away**.

owoy   way   amay   awab   away

Can you write the word **away** with your eyes open and closed?

Extension

• What is the farthest away from you: the Pacific, Indian, or Atlantic Ocean?

"Help, help! Rhyming Rhino gave me more words that end with the same *ay* sound as in **away**. Counting Crow wants me to find two words with two syllables. Can you help me find them?"

tray

pray

okay

stay

today

big

Trace the word **big**.

big big big

Find the box the word **big** fits into. Write **big** in the correct box.

Circle the letters from the alphabet found in the word **big**.

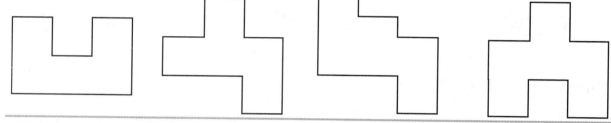

a b c d e f g h i j k l m n o p q r s t u v w x y z

Fill in the missing letters for the word **big**.

b _ g _ i g b i _

b _ _ _ _ g _ i _

Circle the vowel in the word **big**. The vowels are: a, e, i, o, u.

b i g

Fix these words so they spell **big**.

bit bag gib bi dig

big

Put **b** in front of **ig**, and you make the word **big**.
What words do you make when you put these letters in front of **ig**?

b	f	p	r	w	tw

_____ig   _____ig   _____ig

_____ig   _____ig   _____ig

Circle the word **big**.

dig   big   bit   bige   but

Can you write the word **big** with your eyes open and closed?

Extension

• Bus, bike, and car. What is big, bigger, biggest?

"Help, help! Someone put the wrong vowel in **big**! Now there is something crawling on me! What vowel changed **big**?"

bag

beg

big

bog

bug

black

Trace the word **black**.

black black black

Find where the word **black** fits. Write **black** in the correct box.

Circle the letters from the alphabet found in the word **black**.

a b c d e f g h i j k l m n o p q r s t u v w x y z

Fill in the missing letters for the word **black**.

b l _ c k   b l a _ _   b _ _ c k

_ _ a c k   b _ a _ k   _ l _ c _

Circle the vowel in the word **black**. The vowels are: a, e, i, o, u.

b l a c k

Fix these words so they spell **black**.

blak   dlack   block   blakc

black

Put **bl** in front of **ack**, and you make the word **black**.
What words do you make when you put these letters in front of **ack**?

b	l	p	r	s	tr

_____ack   _____ack   _____ack

_____ack   _____ack   _____ack

Circle the word **black**.

block   back   dlack   black   blakc

Can you write the word **black** with your eyes open and closed?

Extension

• Would it be easier to read if the letters were mixed
colors and not all black?

Extra, extra! I have more words
that rhyme with **black**. Can you
read them by yourself?"

black

crack

stack

knack

snack

book

Trace the word **book**.

book   book   book

Find the box the word **book** fits into. Write **book** in the correct box.

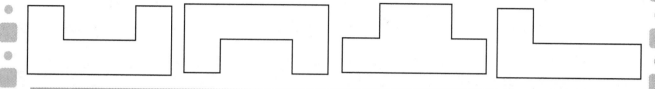

Circle the letters from the alphabet found in the word **book**.

a b c d e f g h i j k l m n o p q r s t u v w x y z

Fill in the missing letters for the word **book**.

b _ o k   b o o _   b _ _ k

_ o o k   b _ o k   _ o _ k

Circle the vowels in the word **book**. The vowels are: a, e, i, o, u.

b   o   o   k

Fix these words so they spell **book**.

bok   boook   dook   koob   buok

book

Put **b** in front of **ook**, and you make the word **book**.
What words do you make when you put these letters in front of **ook**?

c	h	l	n	r	sh

_____ook   _____ook   _____ook

_____ook   _____ook   _____ook

Circle the word **book**.

boook   koob   book   dook

Can you write the word **book** with your eyes open and closed?

Extension

• What type of book helps you spell a word: an encyclopedia or a dictionary?

"Extra, extra! If you add r to **book**, you make a rhyming word that means a small stream. Do you know what it is?"

book

brook

boy

Trace the word **boy**.

boy   boy   boy

Find the box the word **boy** fits into. Write **boy** in the correct box.

Circle the letters from the alphabet found in the word **boy**.

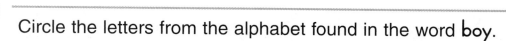

a b c d e f g h i j k l m n o p q r s t u v w x y z

Fill in the missing letters for the word **boy**.

b o _   b _ y   _ o y

b _ _   _ o _   _ _ y

Circle the vowel in the word **boy**. The vowels are: a, e, i, o, u.

b   o   y

Fix these words so they spell **boy**.

bay   yob   booy   bog   doy

boy

Put **b** in front of **oy**, and you make the word **boy**.
What words do you make when you put these letters in front of **oy**?

ah	c	j	s	t	ann

_____oy   _____oy   _____oy

_____oy   _____oy   _____oy

Circle the word **boy**.

doy   boy   bay   yob   hoy

Can you write the word **boy** with your eyes open and closed?

Extension

• Are you a boy or a girl? What is a boy horse: a mare or a stallion?

"Count, count! I want to know which one of these words has two syllables. Put your hand under your chin. Say the word. What word makes your chin hit your hand two times?"

boy

toy

joy

annoy

can

Trace the word **can**.

can   can   can

Find the box the word **can** fits into. Write **can** in the correct box.

Circle the letters from the alphabet found in the word **can**.

a b c d e f g h i j k l m n o p q r s t u v w x y z

Fill in the missing letters for the word **can**.

c _ n   _ a n   c a _

c _ _   _ _ n   _ a _

Circle the vowel in the word **can**. The vowels are: a, e, i, o, u.

c a n

Fix these words so they spell **can**.

cam   con   dan   cann   cna

can

Put **c** in front of **an**, and you make the word **can**.
What words do you make when you put these letters in front of **an**?

b	f	m	p	r	t

_____an _____an _____an

_____an _____an _____an

Circle the word **can**.

cane   cam   con   nac   can

Can you write the word **can** with your eyes open and closed?

Extension
• Can you hop five times on your left foot?

"Extra, extra! I have names that rhyme with **can** and **man** and **fan**. Can you read them?"

Dan

Nan

Jan

Stan

cat

Trace the word **cat**.

cat   cat   cat

Find the box the word **cat** fits into. Write **cat** in the correct box.

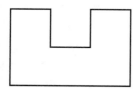 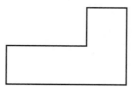 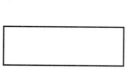 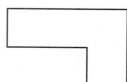

Circle the letters from the alphabet found in the word **cat**.

a b c d e f g h i j k l m n o p q r s t u v w x y z

Fill in the missing letters for the word **cat**.

c _ t   _ a t   c a _

_ _ t   c _ _   _ a _

Circle the vowel in the word **cat**. The vowels are: a, e, i, o, u.

c   a   t

Fix these words so they spell **cat**.

sat   cal   cot   catt   caat

cat

Put c in front of **at**, and you make the word **cat**.
What words do you make when you put these letters in front of **at**?

b	h	m	r	s	th

_____at   _____at   _____at

_____at   _____at   _____at

Circle the word **cat**.

cit   tac   cut   cat   cate

Can you write the word **cat** with your eyes open and closed?

Extension
• What has kittens: a dog or a cat?

"Listen, listen! When a vowel says its name, it is long. Is the vowel in **cat** long?"

c

a

t

could

Trace the word **could**.

could   could   could

Find the box the word **could** fits into. Write **could** in the correct box.

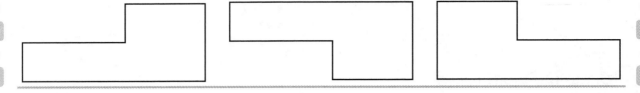

Circle the letters from the alphabet found in the word **could**.

a b c d e f g h i j k l m n o p q r s t u v w x y z

Fill in the missing letters for the word **could**.

c o u l _   c _ _ l d   _ o u _ _

c _ _ _ d   _ u l d   c _ u _ d

Circle the vowels in the word **could**. The vowels are: **a, e, i, o, u.**

c   o   u   l   d

Fix these words so they spell **could**.

coulb   cold   nould   coud   culd

could

Put **c** in front of **ould**, and you make the word **could**.
What words do you make when you put these letters in front of **ould**?

c	w	sh

_____ould   _____ould   _____ould

Circle the word **could**.

cuold   coudl   could   coulb   cold

Can you write the word **could** with your eyes open and closed?

Extension

• If you could ride a horse, camel, or elephant, which
one would you chose?

"Help, help! If *should not* can
change to *shouldn't*, and *would not*
can change to *wouldn't*, what does
could not change to?"

could not

couldn't

did

Trace the word **did**.

did   did   did

Find the box the word **did** fits into. Write **did** in the correct box.

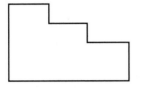 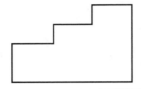 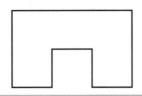 

Circle the letters from the alphabet found in the word **did**.

a b c d e f g h i j k l m n o p q r s t u v w x y z

Fill in the missing letters for the word **did**.

d _ d   _ i d   d i _

d _ _   _ _ d   _ i _

Circle the vowel in the word **did**. The vowels are: a, e, i, o, u.

d   i   d

Fix these words so they spell **did**.

bid   dib   djd   diid   dad

did

Put **d** in front of **id**, and you make the word **did**.
What words do you make when you put these letters in front of **id**?

sl	b	h	k	l	r

____id   ____id   ____id

____id   ____id   ____id

Circle the word **did**.

bib   did   bid   dad   dib

Can you write the word **did** with your eyes open and closed?

Extension

• Did you ever see a monkey?

"Count, count! Does the word **did** have more than one syllable? Put your hand under your chin and say **did**. How many times does your chin hit your hand?"

one

two

three

four

five

dog

Trace the word **dog**.

dog   dog   dog

Find the box the word **dog** fits into. Write **dog** in the correct box.

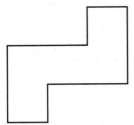 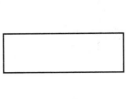 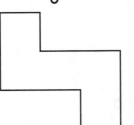 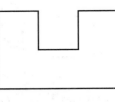

Circle the letters from the alphabet found in the word **dog**.

a b c d e f g h i j k l m n o p q r s t u v w x y z

Fill in the missing letters for the word **dog**.

d _ g   _ o g   d o _
d _ _   _ o _   _ _ g

Circle the vowel in the word **dog**. The vowels are: a, e, i, o, u.

d   o   g

Fix these words so they spell **dog**.

bog   dig   god   dob   dogg

dog

Put **d** in front of **og**, and you make the word **dog**.
What words do you make when you put these letters in front of **og**?

b	f	h	j	l	fr

_____og   _____og   _____og

_____og   _____og   _____og

Circle the word **dog**.

dog   god   dag   bog   doog

Can you write the word **dog** with your eyes open and closed?

Extension

• Does a dog meow or does a dog bark?

"Listen, listen! Long vowels say their names. Short vowels do not. Does the vowel in **dog** say its name? Is it long or short?"

dog

down

Trace the word **down**.

down   down   down

Find the box the word **down** fits into. Write **down** in the correct box.

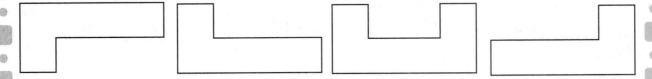

Circle the letters from the alphabet found in the word **down**.

a b c d e f g h i j k l m n o p q r s t u v w x y z

Fill in the missing letters for the word **down**.

d o w _   d _ w n   _ _ w n

_ o w _   d _ w _   d _ _ n

Circle the vowel in the word **down**. The vowels are: a, e, i, o, u.

d o w n

Fix these words so they spell **down**.

bown   domn   dowm   dawn   dow

down

Put **d** in front of **own**, and you make the word **down**.
What words do you make when you put these letters in front of **own**?

g	t	br	cl	cr	fr

_____own   _____own   _____own

_____own   _____own   _____own

Circle the word **down**.

domn   bown   dawn   down   nwod

Can you write the word **down** with your eyes open and closed?

Extension

• What goes up when the rain comes down? An umbrella.

"Help, help! Someone put the word **down** and **town** together. What new word did they make?"

down

town

downtown

each

Trace the word **each**.

each   each   each

Find the box the word **each** fits into. Write **each** in the correct box.

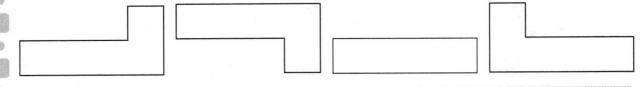

Circle the letters from the alphabet found in the word **each**.

a b c d e f g h i j k l m n o p q r s t u v w x y z

Fill in the missing letters for the word **each**.

e a c _   _ a c h   _ _ c h

e a _ h   _ a _ h   _ a c _

Circle the vowel in the word **each**. The vowels are: a, e, i, o, u.

e   a   c   h

Fix these words so they spell **each**.

aech   eahc   eech   eash   hcae

each

You can make new words by putting letters in front of **each**.
What words do you make when you put these letters in front of **each**?

b	t	p	r	bl	pr

_____each   _____each   _____each

_____each   _____each   _____each

Circle the word **each**.

aech   eech   eacb   oach   each

Can you write the word **each** with your eyes open and closed?

Extension

- If each one of you took two peaches, how many
  peaches would that be?

"Listen, listen! When two vowels go
walking, the first one usually does the
talking. What vowel does the talking
in these words?"

each

beach

teach

peach

reach

end

Trace the word **end**.

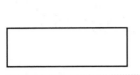　　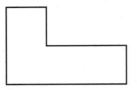　　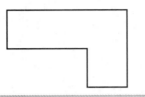　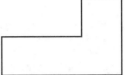

Find the box the word **end** fits into. Write **end** in the correct box.

Circle the letters from the alphabet found in the word **end**.

abcdefghijklmnopqrstuvwxyz

Fill in the missing letters for the word **end**.

e _ d　　　_ n d　　　e _ _

e n _　　　_ n _　　　_ _ d

Circle the vowel in the word **end**. The vowels are: a, e, i, o, u.

e　　n　　d

Fix these words so they spell **end**.

emd　　enb　　and　　emnd　　enbd

end

You can make new words by putting letters in front of **end**.
What words do you make when you put these letters in front of **end**?

b	l	m	t	s	sp

____end   ____end   ____end

____end   ____end   ____end

Circle the word **end**.

emd   enb   and   eup   end

Can you write the word **end** with your eyes open and closed?

Extension

• Does the beginning of a story come at the start or at the end?

"Listen, listen! Detective Dog wants to know if the word **end** has to have the vowel *e*. Can you tell Detective Dog what happens to **end** if we use the vowel *a* instead of *e*?"

end

and

end

and

end

fun

Trace the word **fun**.

fun   fun   fun

Find the box the word **fun** fits into. Write **fun** in the correct box.

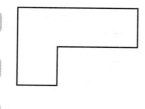 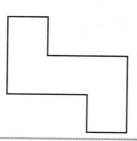 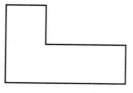 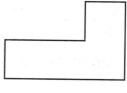

Circle the letters from the alphabet found in the word **fun**.

a b c d e f g h i j k l m n o p q r s t u v w x y z

Fill in the missing letters for the word **fun**.

f _ n   f u _   _ u n
f _ _   _ u _   _ _ n

Circle the vowel in the word **fun**. The vowels are: a, e, i, o, u.

f u n

Fix these words so they spell **fun**.

bun   fum   fan   nuf   fumn

fun

Put f in front of un, and you make the word fun.
What words do you make when you put these letters in front of un?

b	g	r	s	sp	st

_____un   _____un   _____un

_____un   _____un   _____un

Circle the word fun.

fan   bun   fun   sun   nuf

Can you write the word fun with your eyes open and closed?

Extension

• Do you like to have fun in the sun? What is fun to do in the sun?

"Listen, listen! Detective Dog wants to know if the word fun has to have the vowel u. Can you tell Detective Dog what happens to fun if we use the vowels a and i instead of u?"

fun
fan
fin

funny

Trace the word **funny**.

funny   *funny*   *funny*

Find the box the word **funny** fits into. Write **funny** in the correct box.

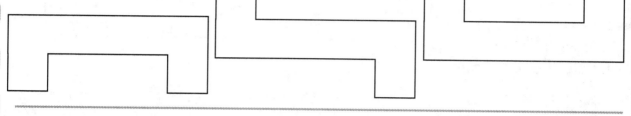

Circle the letters from the alphabet found in the word **funny**.

a b c d e f g h i j k l m n o p q r s t u v w x y z

Fill in the missing letters for the word **funny**.

f u _ _ y   _ u n n _   f _ n _ y

f u n _ _   _ _ _ n y   f _ _ _ y

Circle the vowel in the word **funny**. The vowels are: a, e, i, o, u.

f u n n y

Fix these words so they spell **funny**.

funy   funnny   bunny   fumny   fanny

funny

Put **f** in front of **unny**, and you make the word **funny**.
What words do you make when you put these letters in front of **unny**?

f	s	b	r

_____unny   _____unny

_____unny   _____unny

Circle the word **funny**.

fanny   fumny   fonny   funny   funy

Can you write the word **funny** with your eyes open and closed?

Extension

- Why is **racecar** a funny word? It reads the same backwards and forwards!

"Count, count! Count how many syllables **fun**, **sun**, **bun**, and **run** have when **ny** is added. Put your hand under your chin and say these words. How many times does your chin hit your hand?"

fun

funny

sun

sunny

bun

bunny

run

runny

girl

Trace the word **girl**.

girl　　　girl　　　girl

Find the box the word **girl** fits into. Write **girl** in the correct box.

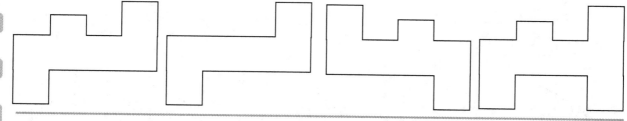

Circle the letters from the alphabet found in the word **girl**.

a b c d e f g h i j k l m n o p q r s t u v w x y z

Fill in the missing letters for the word **girl**.

_ i r l　　　g _ r l　　　g i _ l

g i _ _　　　g _ _ l　　　_ i r _

Circle the vowel in the word **girl**. The vowels are: a, e, i, o, u.

g　i　r　l

Fix these words so they spell **girl**.

gurl　　gilr　　jirl　　ginl　　giiirl

girl

Put g in front of irl, and you make the word girl.
What words do you make when you put these letters in front of irl?

g	sw	tw	wh

____irl   ____irl   ____irl   ____irl

Circle the word girl.

girl   garl   gril   birl   lrig

Can you write the word girl with your eyes open and closed?

Extension

Baby horses and baby zebras are foals.

• Is a girl foal a colt or a filly?
• Is a girl chicken a hen or a rooster?
• Is a girl elephant a cow or a bull?
• Are smaller girl deer bucks or does?

"Help, help! I need to know which one of these words I can add the endings s, ed, and ing to. Can you help me?"

girl
swirl
twirl
whirl

good-by

Trace the word **good-by**.

good-by good-by good-by

Find where the word **good-by** fits. Write **good-by** in the correct box.

Circle the letters from the alphabet found in the word **good-by**.

a b c d e f g h i j k l m n o p q r s t u v w x y z

Fill in the missing letters for the word **good-by**.

g _ _ d- _ _   g _ o _ -b _

_ o d- _ _   _ o o _ - _ y

Circle the vowels in the word **good-by**. The vowels are: a, e, i, o, u, and sometimes y.

g o o d – b y

Fix these words so they spell **good-by**.

goood-by   good-dy   goob-by

good-by

Put **g** in front of **ood**, and you make the word **good**.
Put **b** in front of **y**, and you make the word **by**.
What words do you make when you put these letters in front of **ood** and **y**?

| g | h | st | m | b | fl |

____ood   ____ood   ____y

____ood   ____y   ____y

Circle the word **good-by**.

goob-dy   good-by   goodby

goad-by   good-dy

Can you write the word **good-by** with your eyes open and closed?

Extension

• Do you say "good-by" when you enter or leave a room?

"Help, help! There are two proper ways to write the word **good-by**! What makes them different? Which way do you like best?"

good-by
good-bye

Trace the word **house**.

house   house   house

Find the box the word **house** fits into. Write **house** in the correct box.

Circle the letters from the alphabet found in the word **house**.

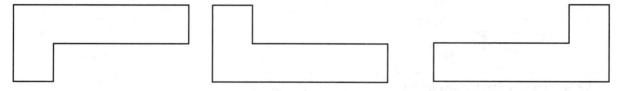

a b c d e f g h i j k l m n o p q r s t u v w x y z

Fill in the missing letters for the word **house**.

_ _ u s e   h _ _ s e

h _ u _ e   _ o s _

Circle the vowels in the word **house**. The vowels are: a, e, i, o, u.

h o u s e

Fix these words so they spell **house**.

huose   hous   bouse   howse   honse

house

Put **h** in front of **ouse**, and you make the word **house**.
What words do you make when you put these letters in front of **ouse**?

h	l	m	sp

_____ouse   _____ouse

_____ouse   _____ouse

Circle the word **house**.

huose   hose   bouse   house   hous

Can you write the word **house** with your eyes open and closed?

Extension

• What is more likely: a house in a mouse or a
  mouse in a house?

"Help, help! If the plural of **louse**
and **mouse** is **lice** and **mice**, what
is the plural of **house**?"

house

hice

houses

how

Trace the word **how**.

how   how   how

Find the box the word **how** fits into. Write **how** in the correct box.

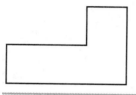 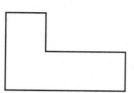 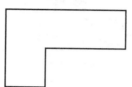 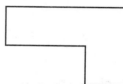

Circle the letters from the alphabet found in the word **how**.

a b c d e f g h i j k l m n o p q r s t u v w x y z

Fill in the missing letters for the word **how**.

h _ w   _ o w   _ o _

h _ _   h o _   _ _ w

Circle the vowel in the word **how**. The vowels are: a, e, i, o, u.

h   o   w

Fix these words so they spell **how**.

hom   haw   bow   who   dow

how

Put **h** in front of **ow**, and you make the word **how**.
What words do you make when you put these letters in front of **ow**?

| b | c | n | s | w | pl |

_____ow _____ow _____ow

_____ow _____ow _____ow

Circle the word **how**.

hom **bow** **haw** **how** **woh**

Can you write the word **how** with your eyes open and closed?

Extension

• How do say your name? How many letters are in
your name?

"Count, count! Put your hand under
your chin. Count the number of
times your chin hits your hand when
you say these words. How many
syllables does each word have?"

how

now

cow

pow

wow

Trace the word **know**.

know   know   know

Find the box the word **know** fits into. Write **know** in the correct box.

Circle the letters from the alphabet found in the word **know**.

abcdefghijklmnopqrstuvwxyz

Fill in the missing letters for the word **know**.

k _ o w   _ n o w   k n _ w

k n _ _   _ _ o w   k _ _ w

Circle the vowel in the word **know**. The vowels are: a, e, i, o, u.

k   n   o   w

Fix these words so they spell **know**.

knom   no   knm   wonk   kmow

know

Put **kn** in front of **ow**, and you make the word **know**.
What words do you make when you put these letters in front of **ow**?

| l | r | gr | sh | sl | sn |

_____ow   _____ow   _____ow

_____ow   _____ow   _____ow

Circle the word **know**.

kmow   knom   know   frow   knaw

Can you write the word **know** with your eyes open and closed?

Extension

• Did you know that the Rafflesia flower can measure three feet across and weigh 15 pounds? It lives in jungles in Southeast Asia.

"Help, help! There is another word that sounds like **know**. It is spelled differently. Does it have a different meaning, too?"

know

no

let

Trace the word **let**.

let　　　　let　　　　let

Find the box the word **let** fits into. Write **let** in the correct box.

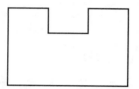 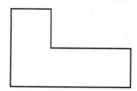 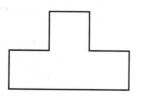 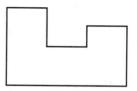

Circle the letters from the alphabet found in the word **let**.

a b c d e f g h i j k l m n o p q r s t u v w x y z

Fill in the missing letters for the word **let**.

l _ t　　　　_ e t　　　　l e _

l _ _　　　　_ e _　　　　_ _ t

Circle the vowel in the word **let**. The vowels are: a, e, i, o, u.

l　e　t

Fix these words so they spell **let**.

leet　　　le　　　lat　　　leaf　　　tel

let

Put l in front of **et**, and you make the word **let**.
What words do you make when you put these letters in front of **et**?

b	j	m	n	p	w

____et   ____et   ____et

____et   ____et   ____et

Circle the word **let**.

lat   lete   tel   let   leg

Can you write the word **let** with your eyes open and closed?

Extension

• Would you let a spider crawl on your arm?

"Listen, listen! The vowel in **let** is short. Does this mean it says its name?"

let

like

Trace the word **like**.

like   like   like

Find the box the word **like** fits into. Write **like** in the correct box.

Circle the letters from the alphabet found in the word **like**.

a b c d e f g h i j k l m n o p q r s t u v w x y z

Fill in the missing letters for the word **like**.

l i k _   _ i k _   l _ k e

l _ _ e   _ i _ e   l _ k _

Circle the vowel in the word **like**. The vowels are: a, e, i, o, u.

l   i   k   e

Fix these words so they spell **like**.

lake   bike   lik   liike   life

like

Put l in front of **ike**, and you make the word **like**.
What words do you make when you put these letters in front of **ike**?

b	h	str	sp

____ike   ____ike

____ike   ____ike

Circle the word **like**.

life   lik   ekil   lake   like

Can you write the word **like** with your eyes open and closed?

Extension

• Do you like to ride a bike? take a hike?

"Listen, Listen! The silent *e* in **like** makes a vowel say its name. Can you find the vowel that says its name?"

like

long

Trace the word long.

long   long   long

Find the box the word long fits into. Write long in the correct box.

Circle the letters from the alphabet found in the word long.

a b c d e f g h i j k l m n o p q r s t u v w x y z

Fill in the missing letters for the word long.

l o n _   l _ n g   _ o _ g

_ o n g   l _ _ g   _ o n _

Circle the vowel in the word long. The vowels are: a, e, i, o, u.

l o n g

Fix these words so they spell long.

lomg   lang   loug   logn   lonh

long

Put l in front of **ong**, and you make the word **long**.
What words do you make when you put these letters in front of **ong**?

l	g	s	pr	wr	str

_____ong   _____ong   _____ong

_____ong   _____ong   _____ong

Circle the word **long**.

lang   lomg   loong   gnol   long

Can you write the word **long** with your eyes open and closed?

Extension

• Is your hand as long as your foot?

"Help, help! I accidentally made an *o* that looks like a *u*. What word did I make instead of **long**?" Hint: you need it to breathe.

long
lung

look

Trace the word **look**.

look   look   look

Find the box the word **look** fits into. Write **look** in the correct box.

Circle the letters from the alphabet found in the word **look**.

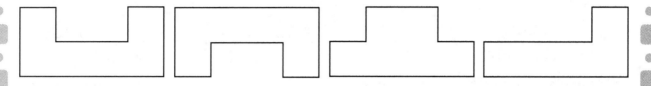

a b c d e f g h i j k l m n o p q r s t u v w x y z

Fill in the missing letters for the word **look**.

l _ o k   _ o o _   l _ _ k

l o _ _   _ o _ k   _ _ _ k

Circle the vowels in the word **look**. The vowels are: a, e, i, o, u.

l   o   o   k

Fix these words so they spell **look**.

lok   loook   loo   loko   kool

look

Put l in front of **ook**, and you make the word **look**.
What words do you make when you put these letters in front of **ook**?

b	c	h	n	t	sh

_____ook   _____ook   _____ook

_____ook   _____ook   _____ook

Circle the word **look**.

loook   kool   look   loak   loom

Can you write the word **look** with your eyes open and closed?

Extension

• What would you use to look at the moon: a microscope or a telescope?

"Help, help! I need to look for a book to help me cook. What do I need?"

look

cook

book

cookbook

make

Trace the word **make**.

make   make   make

Find the box the word **make** fits into. Write **make** in the correct box.

Circle the letters from the alphabet found in the word **make**.

a b c d e f g h i j k l m n o p q r s t u v w x y z

Fill in the missing letters for the word **make**.

m a k _   _ a _ e   _ a k e

m _ _ e   _ _ k e   m _ k _

Circle the vowels in the word **make**. The vowels are: a, e, i, o, u.

m   a   k   e

Fix these words so they spell **make**.

wake   mak   moke   mabe   meka

make

Put **m** in front of **ake**, and you make the word **make**.
What words do you make when you put these letters in front of **ake**?

b	c	f	l	r	qu

_____ake   _____ake   _____ake

_____ake   _____ake   _____ake

Circle the word **make**.

wake   meka   ekam   make   mabe

Can you write the word **make** with your eyes open and closed?

Extension

• Make a silly, a happy, and a sad face. Which one is the most fun to make?

"Listen, listen! The silent *e* in **make** makes a vowel say its name. Can you find the vowel that says its name?"

make

might

Trace the word **might**.

might   might   might

Find the box the word **might** fits into. Write **might** in the correct box.

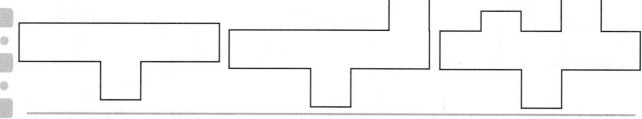

Circle the letters from the alphabet found in the word **might**.

a b c d e f g h i j k l m n o p q r s t u v w x y z

Fill in the missing letters for the word **might**.

m _ g h t   _ _ g h t   _ i _ h t

m i _ _ _   _ i g _ _   m _ _ _ t

Circle the vowel in the word **might**. The vowels are: a, e, i, o, u.

m   i   g   h   t

Fix these words so they spell **might**.

night   mibht   mite   migh   mgiht

might

Put **m** in front of **ight**, and you make the word **might**.
What words do you make when you put these letters in front of **ight**?

f	l	n	r	s	br

____ight   ____ight   ____ight

____ight   ____ight   ____ight

Circle the word **might**.

might   night   mihgt   migh   thgim

Can you write the word **might** with your eyes open and closed?

Extension

• What country or place might you visit one day?

"Extra, extra! Add the letters *h* and *e* to *ight*, and you make another word that rhymes with **might**. If you only put an *e* in front of *ight*, the new word does not rhyme with **might**. It is a number. Do you know what number?"

might
height
eight

---

most

Trace the word **most**.

most   most   most

Find the box the word **most** fits into. Write **most** in the correct box.

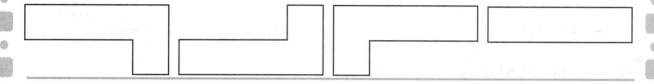

Circle the letters from the alphabet found in the word **most**.

a b c d e f g h i j k l m n o p q r s t u v w x y z

Fill in the missing letters for the word **most**.

m o s _   m o _ _   _ o s _

m o _ t   _ _ s t   m _ _ t

Circle the vowel in the word **most**. The vowels are: a, e, i, o, u.

m   o   s   t

Fix these words so they spell **most**.

nost   must   mots   wost   mist

most

Put **m** in front of **ost**, and you make the word **most**.
What words do you make when you put these letters in front of **ost**?

m	h	p	gh	alm

_____ost   _____ost   _____ost

_____ost   _____ost   _____ost

Circle the word **most**.

most   must   nost   wost   mots

Can you write the word **most** with your eyes open and closed?

Extension

• What would you like most: a swim in the ocean or a
  swim in a pool?

"Count, count! One of these words
has more than one syllable. Put
your hand under your chin and say
the words. On what word does
your chin hit your hand two times?"

most

ghost

post

almost

host

mother

Trace the word **mother**.

mother mother mother

Find the box the word **mother** fits into. Write **mother** in the correct box.

Circle the letters from the alphabet found in the word **mother**.

abcdefghijklmnopqrstuvwxyz

Fill in the missing letters for the word **mother**.

m o t h __ __   m o __ __ e r

m __ t __ e __   __ o __ __ e r

Circle the vowels in the word **mother**. The vowels are: a, e, i, o, u.

m   o   t   h   e   r

Fix these words so they spell **mother**.

mather   moth   wother   moer   other

mother

Put **m** in front of **other**, and you make the word **mother**.
What words do you make when you put these letters in front of **other**?

m	br	an	b

_____other   _____other

_____other   _____other

Circle the word **mother**.

mother   **moter**   **wother**   **motber**

Can you write the word **mother** with your eyes open and closed?

Extension

• Can a mother be a grandmother or a grandfather?

"Count, count! Does **mother** have more than one syllable? Put your hand under your chin and say **mother**. How many times does your chin hit your hand?"

one

two

three

four

five

name

Trace the word **name**.

name   name   name

Find the box the word **name** fits into. Write **name** in the correct box.

Circle the letters from the alphabet found in the word **name**.

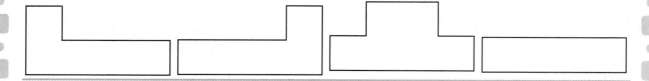

a b c d e f g h i j k l m n o p q r s t u v w x y z

Fill in the missing letters for the word **name**.

n _ m e   n a m _   n _ _ e

n _ _ _   _ _ m e   _ a _ e

Circle the vowels in the word **name**. The vowels are: a, e, i, o, u.

n a m e

Fix these words so they spell **name**.

nam   mane   uame   eman   nawe

name

Put **n** in front of **ame**, and you make the word **name**.
What words do you make when you put these letters in front of **ame**?

c	f	g	l	s	t

_____ame   _____ame   _____ame

_____ame   _____ame   _____ame

Circle the word **name**.

mane   nawe   uame   eman   name

Can you write the word **name** with your eyes open and closed?

Extension

• What is yours, but others use it more than you do?
  Your name!

name

fame

game

lame

same

tame

"Listen, listen! The silent *e* in **name** makes a vowel say its name. What vowel says its **name** in these words?"

night

Trace the word **night**.

night night night

Find the box the word **night** fits into. Write **night** in the correct box.

Circle the letters from the alphabet found in the word **night**.

a b c d e f g h i j k l m n o p q r s t u v w x y z

Fill in the missing letters for the word **night**.

n i _ _ t   _ i _ h _

n _ g _ t   _ _ g h _

Circle the vowel in the word **night**. The vowels are: a, e, i, o, u.

n i g h t

Fix these words so they spell **night**.

might nibht nite nigh ngiht

night

Put **n** in front of **ight**, and you make the word **night**.
What words do you make when you put these letters in front of **ight**?

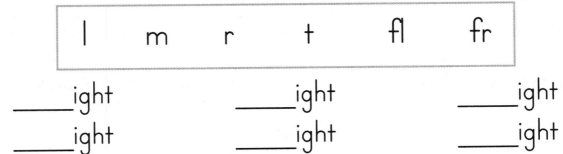

l	m	r	t	fl	fr

____ight   ____ight   ____ight

____ight   ____ight   ____ight

Circle the word **night**.

nibht   might   night   light   nigh   nt

Can you write the word **night** with your eyes open and closed?

Extension

• Do you sleep at night or in the day? What or who might sleep at night?

"Help, help! Someone put the word **to** in front of **night**. What new word did **to** and **night** make?"

to

night

tonight

part

Trace the word **part**.

part   part   part

Find the box the word **part** fits into. Write **part** in the correct box.

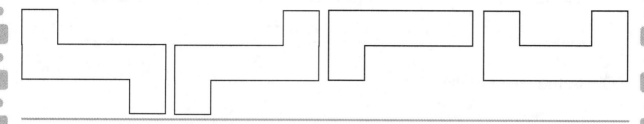

Circle the letters from the alphabet found in the word **part**.

a b c d e f g h i j k l m n o p q r s t u v w x y z

Fill in the missing letters for the word **part**.

p a r _   p _ r t   _ a r _

p a _ t   _ a _ t   p _ r _

Circle the vowel in the word **part**. The vowels are: a, e, i, o, u.

p a r t

Fix these words so they spell **part**.

bart   gart   pant   prt   art

part

Put **p** in front of **art**, and you make the word **part**.
What words do you make when you put these letters in front of **art**?

| p | c | d | t | ap | st |

____art   ____art   ____art

____art   ____art   ____art

Circle the word **part**.

gart   pant   part   trap   port

Can you write the word **part** with your eyes open and closed?

Extension

• What part would you like to act in a play: a donkey,
  a monkey, or a child?

"Help, help! I have a word that
looks like it should rhyme with **part**,
but it does not rhyme with **part**.
What is this word? Hint: It is a
small, hard growth on the skin."

part

wart

play

Trace the word **play**.

play   play   play

Find the box the word **play** fits into. Write **play** in the correct box.

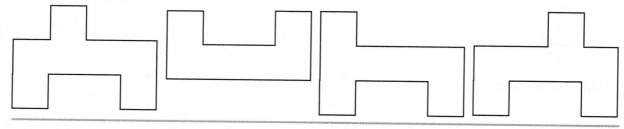

Circle the letters from the alphabet found in the word **play**.

a b c d e f g h i j k l m n o p q r s t u v w x y z

Fill in the missing letters for the word **play**.

p l _ y   p l a _   p _ _ y

p _ _ _   _ _ a y   _ l _ y

Circle the vowel in the word **play**. The vowels are: a, e, i, o, u.

p l a y

Fix these words so they spell **play**.

bart   gart   pant   prt   art

play

Put **pl** in front of **ay**, and you make the word **play**.
What words do you make when you put these letters in front of **ay**?

b	d	h	m	p	s

____ay   ____ay   ____ay

____ay   ____ay   ____ay

Circle the word **play**.

ploy   yalp   paly   blay   play

Can you write the word **play** with your eyes open and closed?

Extension

• How do you play when you are alone? How do you play with friends?

"Help, help! Rhyming Rhino gave me more words that rhyme with play. Counting Crow says two of the words have two syllables. Can you find them? Hint: they start with vowels."

way

away

pray

tray

stay

okay

ran

Trace the word **ran**.

ran   ran   ran

Find the box the word **ran** fits into. Write **ran** in the correct box.

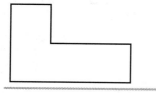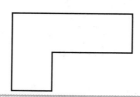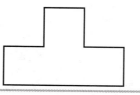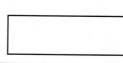

Circle the letters from the alphabet found in the word **ran**.

a b c d e f g h i j k l m n o p q r s t u v w x y z

Fill in the missing letters for the word **ran**.

r _ n   _ a n   r a _

r _ _   _ a _   _ _ n

Circle the vowel in the word **ran**. The vowels are: a, e, i, o, u.

r   a   n

Fix these words so they spell **ran**.

ron   ram   nar   rin   rant

ran

Put **r** in front of **an**, and you make the word **ran**.
What words do you make when you put these letters in front of **an**?

c	f	m	p	sp	th

_____an   _____an   _____an

_____an   _____an   _____an

Circle the word **ran**.

ran   **ram**   **ron**   **rim**   **nar**

Can you write the word **ran** with your eyes open and closed?

Extension

• If a turtle and a rabbit ran a race, who do you think
  would win?

"Listen, listen! Detective Dog wants to
know if the word **ran** has to have the
vowel *a*. Can you tell Detective Dog
what happens to **ran** if we use the
vowel *u* instead of *a*?"

ran

run

ran

run

ran

red

Trace the word **red**.

red   red   red

Find the box the word **red** fits into. Write **red** in the correct box.

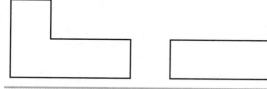 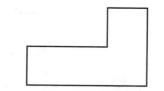 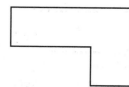

Circle the letters from the alphabet found in the word **red**.

abcdefghijklmnopqrstuvwxyz

Fill in the missing letters for the word **red**.

r _ d   _ e d   r e _

r _ _   _ e _   _ _ d

Circle the vowel in the word **red**. The vowels are: a, e, i, o, u.

r e d

Fix these words so they spell **red**.

reb   rad   der   reed   read

red

Put **r** in front of **ed**, and you make the word **red**.
What words do you make when you put these letters in front of **ed**?

| b | f | l | w | sh | sp |

_____ed   _____ed   _____ed

_____ed   _____ed   _____ed

Circle the word **red**.

read   reb   red   rob   der

Can you write the word **red** with your eyes open and closed?

Extension

• What color do you get if you mix red with yellow?
purple? orange?

"Extra, extra! I have names that rhyme with **red** and **bed** and **led**. Can you read them?"

Ned
Ted
Fred

Trace the word **saw**.

saw saw saw

Find the box the word **saw** fits into. Write **saw** in the correct box.

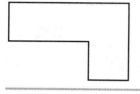 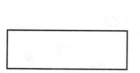 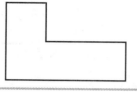 

Circle the letters from the alphabet found in the word **saw**.

abcdefghijklmnopqrstuvwxyz

Fill in the missing letters for the word **saw**.

s _ w   _ a w   s a _

s _ _   _ a _   _ _ w

Circle the vowel in the word **saw**. The vowels are: a, e, i, o, u.

s a w

Fix these words so they spell **saw**.

saaw   sam   was   sawm   sw

saw

Put **s** in front of **aw**, and you make the word **saw**.

What words do you make when you put these letters in front of **aw**?

j	l	p	r	cl	str

_____aw   _____aw   _____aw

_____aw   _____aw   _____aw

Circle the word **saw**.

saw   **sam**   **san**   **sew**   **was**

Can you write the word **saw** with your eyes open and closed?

Extension

• If you saw crows and owls, which ones would say "Caw"? How about "Hoot"?

"Help, help! Someone wrote the word **saw** backwards! Written backwards, **saw** is the word **was**. Which words are **saw**? Which words are **was**?"

saw

was

was

saw

saw

was

school

Trace the word **school**.

school   school   school

Find the box the word **school** fits into. Write **school** in the correct box.

Circle the letters from the alphabet found in the word **school**.

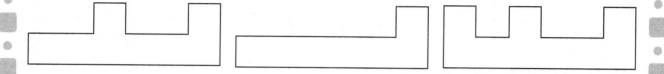

a b c d e f g h i j k l m n o p q r s t u v w x y z

Fill in the missing letters for the word **school**.

s _ h o _ l   _ c _ o o l

s _ _ o o l   _ c _ o _ l

Circle the vowels in the word **school**. The vowels are: a, e, i, o, u.

s c h o o l

Fix these words so they spell **school**.

shool   schooool   skool   schol   scool

school

Put **sch** in front of **ool**, and you make the word **school**.

What words do you make when you put these letters in front of **ool**?

| p | c | f | t | sp | st |

____ool   ____ool   ____ool

____ool   ____ool   ____ool

Circle the word **school**.

shool   scbool   schol   schoool   school

Can you write the word **school** with your eyes open and closed?

Extension

• What is your favorite thing about school?

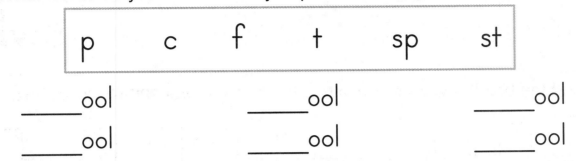

"Extra, extra! I have two words that rhyme with **school**, **pool**, and **tool**. They are spelled differently. Can you read them?"

school

pool

tool

rule

mule

see

Trace the word **see**.

see   see   see

Find the box the word **see** fits into. Write **see** in the correct box.

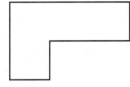 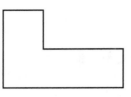 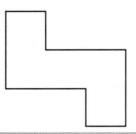 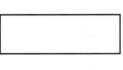

Circle the letters from the alphabet found in the word **see**.

abcdefghijklmnopqrstuvwxyz

Fill in the missing letters for the word **see**.

s e _   _ e e   s _ e

s _ _   _ e _   _ _ e

Circle the vowel in the word **see**. The vowels are: **a, e, i, o, u.**

s   e   e

Fix these words so they spell **see**.

se   cee   sea   seee   sse

see

Put **s** in front of **ee**, and you make the word **see**.

What words do you make when you put these letters in front of **ee**?

b	f	fr	kn	tr	thr

_____ee   _____ee   _____ee

_____ee   _____ee   _____ee

Circle the word **see**.

sea   seem   se   ees   see

Can you write the word **see** with your eyes open and closed?

Extension

• Can you see a tree from where you are sitting? Can you see a bee?

"Extra, extra! I have one word that sounds exactly like **see**. I have five words that rhyme with **see**. All the words are spelled a little differently. Can you read these words? What do the words mean?"

see

sea

be

he

me

we

she

she

Trace the word **she**.

she   she   she

Find the box the word **she** fits into. Write **she** in the correct box.

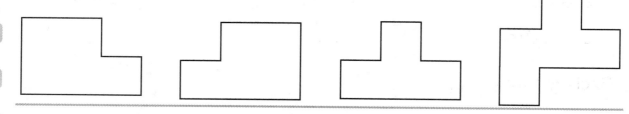

Circle the letters from the alphabet found in the word **she**.

a b c d e f g h i j k l m n o p q r s t u v w x y z

Fill in the missing letters for the word **she**.

s __ e   __ h e   s h __

s __ __   __ h __   __ __ e

Circle the vowel in the word **she**. The vowels are: a, e, i, o, u.

s   h   e

Fix these words so they spell **she**.

sh   shee   he   see   sbe

she

Put **sh** in front of **e**, and you make the word **she**.
What words do you make when you put these letters in front of **e**?

sh	b	h	m	w

_____e   _____e   _____e

_____e   _____e

Circle the word **she**.

sha   she   sbe   ehs   he

Can you write the word **she** with your eyes open and closed?

Extension

• Is a girl a "she" or a "he"?

"Extra, extra! I have words that rhyme with **she** and **he** and **me**. They are spelled a little differently. Can you read them?"

she

he

me

see

bee

sing

Trace the word **sing**.

sing   sing   sing

Find the box the word **sing** fits into. Write **sing** in the correct box.

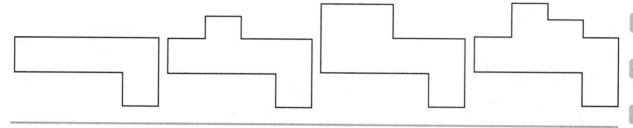

Circle the letters from the alphabet found in the word **sing**.

a b c d e f g h i j k l m n o p q r s t u v w x y z

Fill in the missing letters for the word **sing**.

_ i n g   s i n _   s _ n g

s i _ _   _ _ n g   s _ _ g

Circle the vowel in the word **sing**. The vowels are: a, e, i, o, u.

s   i   n   g

Fix these words so they spell **sing**.

sin   sang   simg   siing   sinp

sing

Put **s** in front of **ing**, and you make the word **sing**.
What words do you make when you put these letters in front of **ing**?

k	r	w	br	st	th

____ing   ____ing   ____ing

____ing   ____ing   ____ing

Circle the word **sing**.

sting   song   sinp   sing   simg

Can you write the word **sing** with your eyes open and closed?

Extension
• What song do you like to sing?

"Help, help! A little puppy put the letters *i*, *n*, and *g* at the end of sing, **bring**, and **sting**. Can you read the words now?"

sing

singing

bring

bringing

sting

stinging

sit

Trace the word **sit**.

sit   sit   sit

Find the box the word **sit** fits into. Write **sit** in the correct box.

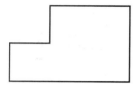  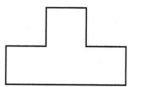 

Circle the letters from the alphabet found in the word **sit**.

a b c d e f g h i j k l m n o p q r s t u v w x y z

Fill in the missing letters for the word **sit**.

s _ t   _ i t   s i _

s _ _   _ i _   _ _ t

Circle the vowel in the word **sit**. The vowels are: a, e, i, o, u.

s   i   t

Fix these words so they spell **sit**.

cit   sat   sil   sitt   siit

sit

Put **s** in front of **it**, and you make the word **sit**.
What words do you make when you put these letters in front of **it**?

b	f	h	p	qu	sp

___it   ___it   ___it

___it   ___it   ___it

Circle the word **sit**.

sit   sat   sut   tis   sot

Can you write the word **sit** with your eyes open and closed?

Extension

• Do you sit down or stand up on a chair?

"Extra, extra! I have a word that rhymes with **sit** and **hit** and **bit**. It is spelled a little differently. Can you read it?"

sit

hit

bit

mitt

some

Trace the word **some**.

some   some   some

Find the box the word **some** fits into. Write **some** in the correct box.

Circle the letters from the alphabet found in the word **some**.

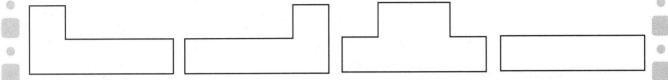

a b c d e f g h i j k l m n o p q r s t u v w x y z

Fill in the missing letters for the word **some**.

s _ m e   _ o m e   s o m _

s _ m _   _ o _ e   s _ _ e

Circle the vowel in the word **some**. The vowels are: a, e, i, o, u.

s o m e

Fix these words so they spell **some**.

mose   same   sone   sowe   som

some

Put **s** in front of **ome**, and you make the word **some**.
What words do you make when you put these letters in front of **ome**?

s	c

_____ome   _____ome

Circle the word **some**.

sone   some   emos   same   somm

Can you write the word **some** with your eyes open and closed?

Extension

• Would you like some eggs or some chickens?

"Extra, extra! I have a word that rhymes with **some** and **come**. It is spelled a little differently. Can you read it?"

some

come

from

---

stop

Trace the word **stop**.

stop   stop   stop

Find the box the word **stop** fits into. Write **stop** in the correct box.

Circle the letters from the alphabet found in the word **stop**.

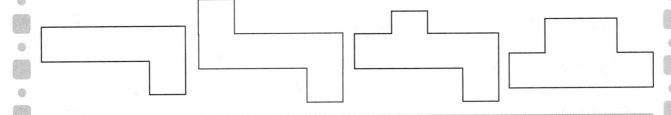

a b c d e f g h i j k l m n o p q r s t u v w x y z

Fill in the missing letters for the word **stop**.

s _ o p   _ t o p   s _ _ p

s t _ _   _ t _ p   _ t o _

Circle the vowel in the word **stop**. The vowels are: a, e, i, o, u.

s   t   o   p

Fix these words so they spell **stop**.

top   stup   stob   stod   stoupb

stop

Put **st** in front of **op**, and you make the word **stop**.

What words do you make when you put these letters in front of **op**?

c	h	m	t	cr	sh

_____op _____op _____op

_____op _____op _____op

Circle the word **stop**.

stup   stob   stod   stip   stop

Can you write the word **stop** with your eyes open and closed?

Extension

• Do you stop at a green light or a red light?

"Listen, listen! When a vowel says its name, it is long. Is the vowel in **stop** long?"

stop

take

Trace the word **take**.

take   take   take

Find the box the word **take** fits into. Write **take** in the correct box.

Circle the letters from the alphabet found in the word **take**.

a b c d e f g h i j k l m n o p q r s t u v w x y z

Fill in the missing letters for the word **take**.

_ a k e   _ _ k e   t _ _ e

t a _ _   _ a _ e   t _ k _

Circle the vowels in the word **take**. The vowels are: a, e, i, o, u.

t a k e

Fix these words so they spell **take**.

tak   fake   toke   takke   tace

take

Put t in front of **ake**, and you make the word **take**.
What words do you make when you put these letters in front of **ake**?

m	w	br	fl	sh	sn

____ake   ____ake   ____ake

____ake   ____ake   ____ake

Circle the word **take**.

tak   tike   take   ekat   talk

Can you write the word **take** with your eyes open and closed?

Extension

• Do you take a bus when you go to school?

"Listen, listen! The silent *e* in **take** makes a vowel say its name. Can you find the vowel that says its name?"

take

tell

Trace the word **tell**.

tell   tell   tell

Find the box the word **tell** fits into. Write **tell** in the correct box.

Circle the letters from the alphabet found in the word **tell**.

a b c d e f g h i j k l m n o p q r s t u v w x y z

Fill in the missing letters for the word **tell**.

t _ l l   _ e l l   t e _ _

t _ _ l   t _ _ l   _ _ l l

Circle the vowel in the word **tell**. The vowels are: a, e, i, o, u.

t e l l

Fix these words so they spell **tell**.

tel   tall   telll   let   tele

tell

Put t in front of **ell**, and you make the word **tell**.
What words do you make when you put these letters in front of **ell**?

b	c	f	s	w	sp

____ell   ____ell   ____ell

____ell   ____ell   ____ell

Circle the word **tell**.

telll tall tell llet till

Can you write the word **tell** with your eyes open and closed?

Extension

• Can you tell me how old you are? Can you tell me
  when your birthday is?

"Help, help! Two of the **tell** rhyming
words sound the same. They are
spelled differently. Do they have
the same meaning?"

tell

sell

cell

thank

Trace the word **thank**.

thank   thank   thank

Find the box the word **thank** fits into. Write **thank** in the correct box.

Circle the letters from the alphabet found in the word **thank**.

a b c d e f g h i j k l m n o p q r s t u v w x y z

Fill in the missing letters for the word **thank**.

_ h a n _   _ _ a n k   t h _ n k

t h a _ _   t h _ _ _   t _ a _ k

Circle the vowel in the word **thank**. The vowels are: a, e, i, o, u.

t h a n k

Fix these words so they spell **thank**.

tank   thunk   than   thamb   knaht

thank

Put **th** in front of **ank**, and you make the word **thank**.
What words do you make when you put these letters in front of **ank**?

b	r	s	cr	pr	sp

_____ank   _____ank   _____ank

_____ank   _____ank   _____ank

Circle the word **thank**.

thunk   thamk   tank   think   thank

Can you write the word **thank** with your eyes open and closed?

Extension

• Do you say "Thank you" or "Excuse me" when given something?

"Help, help! I don't know what word usually goes with the word **thank**. Can you help me?"

thank me

thank he

thank she

thank you

that

Trace the word **that**.

that   that   that

Find the box the word **that** fits into. Write **that** in the correct box.

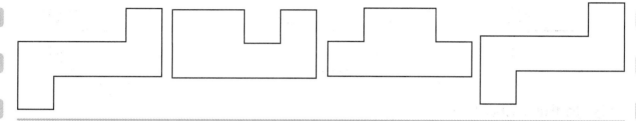

Circle the letters from the alphabet found in the word **that**.

a b c d e f g h i j k l m n o p q r s t u v w x y z

Fill in the missing letters for the word **that**.

t h _ t   t h _ _   _ h _ t

t _ a _   _ _ a t   t _ _ t

Circle the vowel in the word **that**. The vowels are: a, e, i, o, u.

t h a t

Fix these words so they spell **that**.

hat   tbat   thit   tht   than

that

Put th in front of at, and you make the word that.
What words do you make when you put these letters in front of at?

| b | c | h | s | ch | fl |

____at   ____at   ____at

____at   ____at   ____at

Circle the word that.

hat   tbat   that   thot   taht

Can you write the word that with your eyes open and closed?

Extension
• That creature has eight legs. Could it be a spider or
  a centipede?

"Help, Help! Rhyming Rhino says
one of these words does not rhyme
with that. Can you help me find it?"

that

cat

pat

rat

what

sat

then

Trace the word **then**.

then then then

Find the box the word **then** fits into. Write **then** in the correct box.

Circle the letters from the alphabet found in the word **then**.

a b c d e f g h i j k l m n o p q r s t u v w x y z

Fill in the missing letters for the word **then**.

_ h e n t h e _ t _ e n

t h _ _ _ _ e n t _ _ n

Circle the vowel in the word **then**. The vowels are: a, e, i, o, u.

t h e n

Fix these words so they spell **then**.

than tben neht them thm

then

Put **th** in front of **en**, and you make the word **then**.
What words do you make when you put these letters in front of **en**?

h	m	p	t	wh	wr

_____en   _____en   _____en

_____en   _____en   _____en

Circle the word **then**.

than   them   neht   then   thene

Can you write the word **then** with your eyes open and closed?

Extension
- If you walked one mile (1.6 kilometers), would you be tired?

"Listen, listen! Detective Dog wants to know if the word **then** has to have the vowel **e**. Can you tell Detective Dog what happens to **then** if we use the vowel **a** instead of **e**?"

then

than

then

than

then

thing

Trace the word **thing**.

thing   thing   thing

Find the box the word **thing** fits into. Write **thing** in the correct box.

Circle the letters from the alphabet found in the word **thing**.

a b c d e f g h i j k l m n o p q r s t u v w x y z

Fill in the missing letters for the word **thing**.

t h _ n _   t _ _ n g   _ _ i n g

t h _ _ g   t _ i n _   _ h _ n _

Circle the vowel in the word **thing**. The vowels are: a, e, i, o, u.

t h i n g

Fix these words so they spell **thing**.

thng   ting   thinb   thimg   thjng

thing

Put **th** in front of **ing**, and you make the word **thing**.
What words do you make when you put these letters in front of **ing**?

r	s	w	br	fl	st

_____ing   _____ing   _____ing

_____ing   _____ing   _____ing

Circle the word **thing**.

thinb   thign   thing   thimg   thin

Can you write the word **thing** with your eyes open and closed?

Extension

• What thing might change into a butterfly: a caterpillar
  or a camel?

"Count, count! Add the word **some**
to **thing** and make a new word. How
many syllables does the new word
have? To count syllables, put your
hand under your chin. Count how
many times your chin hits your hand
when you say the word."

some

thing

something

this

Trace the word **this**.

this   this   this

Find the box the word **this** fits into. Write **this** in the correct box.

Circle the letters from the alphabet found in the word **this**.

a b c d e f g h i j k l m n o p q r s t u v w x y z

Fill in the missing letters for the word **this**.

t h _ s   _ _ i s   t h i _

t _ _ s   t _ i _   _ h i s

Circle the vowel in the word **this**. The vowels are: a, e, i, o, u.

t h i s

Fix these words so they spell **this**.

tis   his   thi   thsi   tbis

this

Put **th** in front of **is**, and you make the word **this**.

There are other words that rhyme with the word **this**. They are spelled a little differently. What rhyming words do you make when you put these letters in front of **is** and **iss**?

th	h	k	m

____is   ____iss

____iss   ____iss

Circle the word **this**.

thas   this   tbis   ths   thias

Can you write the word **this** with your eyes open and closed?

Extension

• Is any day this month a special day for you?

"Listen, listen! Do you hear any long vowels when you say these words that rhyme with **this**? Long vowels say their names."

this

kiss

miss

hiss

time

Trace the word **time**.

time   time   time

Find the box the word **time** fits into. Write **time** in the correct box.

Circle the letters from the alphabet found in the word **time**.

a b c d e f g h i j k l m n o p q r s t u v w x y z

Fill in the missing letters for the word **time**.

t i m _   t _ m e   _ i m e

t _ _ e   _ i _ e   _ _ m e

Circle the vowels in the word **time**. The vowels are: a, e, i, o, u.

t   i   m   e

Fix these words so they spell **time**.

tine   tame   tim   temi   tme

time

Put t in front of **ime**, and you make the word **time**.
What words do you make when you put these letters in front of **ime**?

t	d	l	cr	pr	sl

_____ime   _____ime   _____ime

_____ime   _____ime   _____ime

Circle the word **time**.

time   tine   tame   emit   tim

Can you write the word **time** with your eyes open and closed?

Extension

• What time do you get up? What time is your bedtime?

time

dime

lime

crime

prime

"Listen, listen! The silent *e* in **time** makes a vowel say its name. Does the same vowel say its name in all the rhyming words?"

told

Trace the word **told**.

told   **told**   **told**

Find the box the word **told** fits into. Write **told** in the correct box.

Circle the letters from the alphabet found in the word **told**.

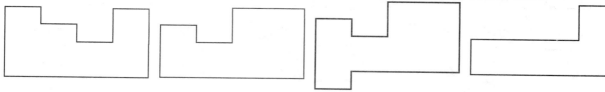

a b c d e f g h i j k l m n o p q r s t u v w x y z

Fill in the missing letters for the word **told**.

t o l _   t o _ _   _ o l d

t _ l _   _ o _ d   _ _ l d

Circle the vowel in the word **told**. The vowels are: a, e, i, o, u.

t o l d

Fix these words so they spell **told**.

tolb   teld   todl   toald   td

told

Put t in front of **old**, and you make the word **told**.
What words do you make when you put these letters in front of **old**?

b	c	f	g	h	s

____old   ____old   ____old

____old   ____old   ____old

Circle the word **told**.

tolb   todl   told   tuld   fold

Can you write the word **told** with your eyes open and closed?

Extension

• Were you ever told, "It is cold! Put on your jacket"?

"Listen, listen! When a vowel says its name, it is long. Are the vowels in these words long?"

told

old

sold

fold

cold

up

Trace the word **up**.

up   up   up

Find the box the word **up** fits into. Write **up** in the correct box.

Circle the letters from the alphabet found in the word **up**.

a b c d e f g h i j k l m n o p q r s t u v w x y z

Fill in the missing letters for the word **up**.

u _   _ p

_ p   u _

Circle the vowel in the word **up**. The vowels are: a, e, i, o, u.

u   p

Fix these words so they spell **up**.

ub   pu   upp   uupp   ud

up

You can make new words by putting letters in front of **up**.
What words do you make when you put these letters in front of **up**?

c	p	s

_____up   _____up   _____up

Circle the word **up**.

ud   ub   up   upp   ap

Can you write the word **up** with your eyes open and closed?

Extension

- Would you like to go up in the air in a plane or a balloon?
- If you put your hand up high, is it above your head or below your feet?
- When do you jump up, and when do you jump down?
- If someone says they are feeling up, do you think they are sad or happy?

"Listen, listen! Long vowels say their names. Short vowels do not. Does the vowel in **up** say its name? Is it long or short?"

up

what

Trace the word **what**.

what   what   what

Find the box the word **what** fits into. Write **what** in the correct box.

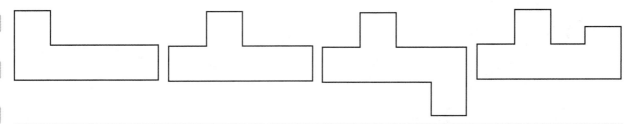

Circle the letters from the alphabet found in the word **what**.

a b c d e f g h i j k l m n o p q r s t u v w x y z

Fill in the missing letters for the word **what**.

| w h a _ | _ h a t | w _ a t |
| w h _ _ | w _ _ t | _ _ a t |

Circle the vowel in the word **what**. The vowels are: a, e, i, o, u.

w   h   a   t

Fix these words so they spell **what**.

hat   wat   tahw   whot   waht

what

Circle the word **what**.

whot   what   mhat   waht   wbat

Can you write the word **what** with your eyes open and closed?

Extension

- What should you say when a tiger holds the door open for you: "Please" or "Thank you"?
- What should you say when you bump into an elephant: "Excuse me" or "Oops"?
- What should you say when you are introduced to a green octopus: "Are you ill?" or "It's very nice to meet you"?
- What should you say when an enormous lion tells you that the word "what" has two syllables: "I believe you are mistaken," or "I agree"?

"Help, help! I need to know what happened to the word **what**. What letter did it lose? Can you read what the word **what** became?"

what

hat

when

Trace the word **when**.

when   when   when

Find the box the word **when** fits into. Write **when** in the correct box.

Circle the letters from the alphabet found in the word **when**.

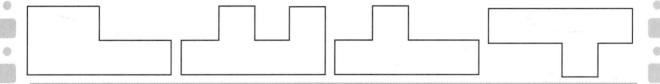

a b c d e f g h i j k l m n o p q r s t u v w x y z

Fill in the missing letters for the word **when**.

_ h e n   w h e _   _ _ e n

w h _ _   _ h e n   w _ _ n

Circle the vowel in the word **when**. The vowels are: a, e, i, o, u.

w   h   e   n

Fix these words so they spell **when**.

whan   mhen   nehw   whem   whm

when

Put **wh** in front of **en**, and you make the word **when**.
What words do you make when you put these letters in front of **en**?

wh	h	m	p	t	th

_____en   _____en   _____en

_____en   _____en   _____en

Circle the word **when**.

what   where   when   why   were

Can you write the word **when** with your eyes open and closed?

Extension

• When do you eat breakfast: in the morning or in the evening?

"Extra, extra! "I have a lot of words that rhyme with **when**. They are spelled a little differently. Can you read them?"

when

ten

hen

Ben

Ken

where

Trace the word **where**.

where   where   where

Find the box the word **where** fits into. Write **where** in the correct box.

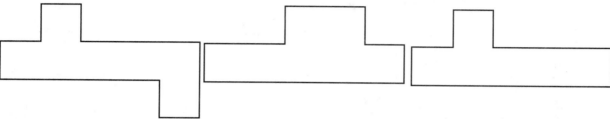

Circle the letters from the alphabet found in the word **where**.

a b c d e f g h i j k l m n o p q r s t u v w x y z

Fill in the missing letters for the word **where**.

w h _ r _   _ _ e r e   w _ e _ e

w h e _ _   _ h _ r _   w h _ _ _

Circle the vowels in the word **where**. The vowels are: a, e, i, o, u.

w h e r e

Fix these words so they spell **where**.

wher   mhere   wbere   here   were

where

Put **wh** in front of **ere**, and you make the word **where**.
What words do you make when you put these letters in front of **ere**?

wh	th
_____ere	_____ere

Circle the word **where**.

where   wheer   mhere   wher   wbere

Can you write the word **where** with your eyes open and closed?

Extension
- Where do you live: on Earth or Jupiter?
- Where is your nose: on your hand or on your face?
- Where do you buy food: in the store or in the library?
- Where is the letter "w" in the alphabet: near the beginning or the end?

"Help, Help! There is another word that sounds exactly like **where**. Can you hear it and find it in this sentence?"
Where are you going to wear a bathing suit?

who

Trace the word **who**.

who   who   who

Find the box the word **who** fits into. Write **who** in the correct box.

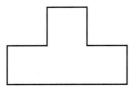 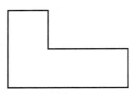 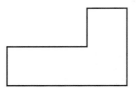 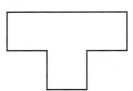

Circle the letters from the alphabet found in the word **who**.

a b c d e f g h i j k l m n o p q r s t u v w x y z

Fill in the missing letters for the word **who**.

w h _   w _ o   _ h o

w _ _   _ h _   _ _ o

Circle the vowel in the word **who**. The vowels are: a, e, i, o, u.

w   h   o

Fix these words so they spell **who**.

wh   wbo   whoo   wo   mho

who

Put **wh** in front of **o**, and you make the word **who**.
What words do you make when you put these letters in front of **o**?

wh	**t**

_____o   _____o

Circle the word **who**.

mho   who   wbo   whoo   hoo

Can you write the word **who** with your eyes open and closed?

Extension

- Who says, "Moo," a cow or a horse?
- Who works with animals: a zoologist or a pediatrician?
- Who studies dinosaurs: an oceanographer or a paleontologist?
- Who designs buildings: an architect or a dentist?
- Who studies trees: a forester or an astronomer?

who

what

where

when

why

"Help, help! I can't tell all these **wh** words apart. Can you tell me what makes **who** different from the other **wh** words?"

why

Trace the word **why**.

why   why   why

Find the box the word **why** fits into. Write **why** in the correct box.

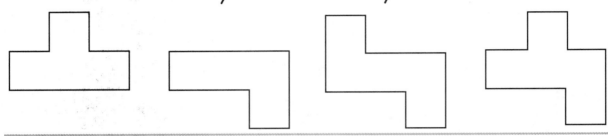

Circle the letters from the alphabet found in the word **why**.

abcdefghijklmnopqrstuvwxyz

Fill in the missing letters for the word **why**.

w _ y   _ h y   w h _

w _ _   _ h _   _ _ y

Circle the vowel in the word **why**. The vowels are: **a, e, i, o, u,** and sometimes **y**.

w   h   y

Fix these words so they spell **why**.

wy   mhy   wh   wby   way

why

Put **wh** in front of **y**, and you make the word **why**.
What words do you make when you put these letters in front of **y**?

| b | m | cr | fr | sp | tr |

_____y   _____y   _____y

_____y   _____y   _____y

Circle the word **why**.

mhy   why   wby   yhw   whiy

Can you write the word **why** with your eyes open and closed?

Extension

• Why do we have teeth?

"Listen, listen! The **y** in **why** and these other rhyming words say the name of another vowel. What vowel name do they say?"

my

by

cry

fry

spy

try

will

Trace the word will.

will   will   will

Find the box the word will fits into. Write will in the correct box.

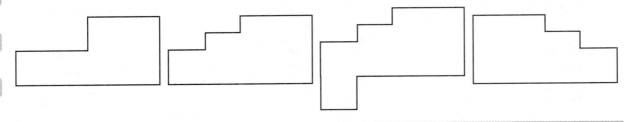

Circle the letters from the alphabet found in the word will.

a b c d e f g h i j k l m n o p q r s t u v w x y z

Fill in the missing letters for the word will.

w _ l l   w i _ l   _ i l l

w _ l _   _ i _ l   _ _ l l

Circle the vowel in the word will. The vowels are: a, e, i, o, u.

w i l l

Fix these words so they spell will.

wil   willl   mill   wall   wlil

will

Put **w** in front of **ill**, and you make the word **will**.
What words do you make when you put these letters in front of **ill**?

f	h	k	p	sp	st

____ill   ____ill   ____ill

____ill   ____ill   ____ill

Circle the word **will**.

wall   mill   wil   will   wlil

Can you write the word **will** with your eyes open and closed?

Extension

• What will you pour your drink into: a plate, cup, or spoon?

"Extra, Extra! I have more words that rhyme with the word **will**. Can you read them?"

will

bill

ill

grill

skill

wish

Trace the word **wish**.

wish   wish   wish

Find the box the word **wish** fits into. Write **wish** in the correct box.

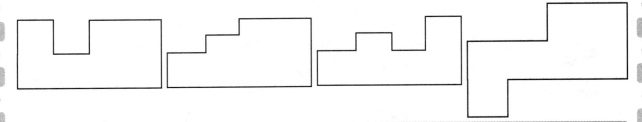

Circle the letters from the alphabet found in the word **wish**.

a b c d e f g h i j k l m n o p q r s t u v w x y z

Fill in the missing letters for the word **wish**.

w _ s h   w i s _   _ i s h

w i _ _   _ i h _   w _ _ h

Circle the vowel in the word **wish**. The vowels are: a, e, i, o, u.

w   i   s   h

Fix these words so they spell **wish**.

wash   wich   mish   wsh   wihs

wish

Put **w** in front of **ish**, and you make the word **wish**.
What words do you make when you put these letters in front of **ish**?

w	d	f	sw

_____ish   _____ish

_____ish   _____ish

Circle the word **wish**.

mish   wash   wihs   wish   wisb

Can you write the word **wish** with your eyes open and closed?

Extension

• Do you ever wish that you could visit a desert, a rain forest, or an iceberg?

"Count, count! Two of these **wish** words have two syllables. Put your hand under your chin. Count how many times your chin hits your hand when you say these words. Can you find the two-syllable words?"

wish

wishes

wished

wishing

would

Trace the word **would**.

would   would   would

Find the box the word **would** fits into. Write **would** in the correct box.

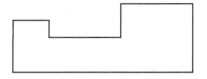   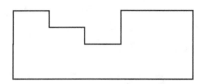   

Circle the letters from the alphabet found in the word **would**.

a b c d e f g h i j k l m n o p q r s t u v w x y z

Fill in the missing letters for the word **would**.

_ _ u l d   w _ _ l d   w o u _ _

w _ _ _ d   _ u l _   w _ u _ d

Circle the vowels in the word **would**. The vowels are: a, e, i, o, u.

w o u l d

Fix these words so they spell **would**.

woulb   wold   mould   woud   wuld

would

Put **w** in front of **ould**, and you make the word **would**.
What words do you make when you put these letters in front of **ould**?

w	c	sh

_____ould   _____ould   _____ould

Circle the word **would**.

would   wonld   mould   woulb   wold

Can you write the word **would** with your eyes open and closed?

Extension

• If you could, would you go to Mars or to the Moon?

"Extra, extra! I have a word that doesn't just rhyme with **would**. It sounds exactly like **would**! It is spelled differently. Do you know what it means?"

would

wood

New Word Form

Name: _____ Date: _____

(write the new word here)

Trace the word.

(Write the new word three times so it can be traced.)

Find the box the word fits into.

(Make three boxes. Only one box should fit your new word shape.)

Circle the letters from the alphabet found in the new word.

a b c d e f g h i j k l m n o p q r s t u v w x y z

Fill in the missing letters.

(Write the word four times, leaving out different letters each time.)

Circle the vowels in the new word. The vowels are: a, e, i, o, u.

(Write the new word.)

Fix these words so they spell the new word correctly.

(Write the word four times. Spell the word incorrectly each time so it can be fixed.)

New Word Form *(cont.)*

Put new letters in front of your new word ending to make new words.

(List, if any, new letters you could put on your new word ending to make new words. For some words, this exercise will not work. You may leave it blank.)

(Write your word ending after the blank for the new letters.)

Circle the new word.

(Write three words. Only one should be the new word spelled correctly.)

Can you write the new word with your eyes open and closed?

Extension

(Write or dictate a question using the new word.)

(Write or dictate something you think Rhyming Rhino, Counting Crow, Vowel Vixen, or Detective Dog would like to say.)

Flash Cards

all	and
are	around
away	big
black	book
boy	can

Flash Cards *(cont.)*

cat	could
did	dog
down	each
end	fun
funny	

Flash Cards *(cont.)*

girl	good-by
house	how
know	let
like	long
look	

Flash Cards *(cont.)*

make	might
most	mother
name	night
part	play
ran	

Flash Cards

red	saw
school	see
she	sing
sit	some
stop	

    142

Flash Cards (cont.)

take	tell
thank	that
then	thing
this	time
told	

Flash Cards _(cont.)_

up	what
when	where
who	why
will	wish
would	